13 Sculptures
Children Should Know

Angela Wenzel

PRESTEL
Munich · Berlin · London · New York

Contents

What is a sculpture? The word "sculpture" comes from the Latin word "sculpere," which means "to chisel" or "to carve." In this book you'll find sculptures carved of wood and stone, but also works of art made of gold, sewn out of fabric, or constructed of earth. These creations come from various parts of the world, but they all have one thing in common: they are three-dimensional objects that take up space. Some more, some less, let them surprise you! A timeline will help you arrange the works from the oldest to the newest. Would you like to know more about a sculpture or an artist? Then the tips for further reading or surfing on the internet will assist you as well. For more fun, there are short quiz questions and instructions to help you understand the art you have seen and to create your own art. So have fun and be creative!

Technical terms* are explained here.

264–146 BC Punic Wars fought between Carthage
(an empire based in northern Africa) and ancient Rome

202 BC Hannibal's army is defeated by the Romans
218 BC Hannibal crosses the Alps and invades Italy
Hannibal 246–182 BC

around 250 BC Greek scientist Archimedes discovers the law of buoyancy, or why objects float in water
222 BC The Romans conquer Mediolarum, now the city of Milan, and control Northern Italy

270 BC   265   260   255   250   245   240   235   230   225   220   200

The figure of Nike

is pieced together from fragments discovered by French researchers in 1863 on the island of Samothrace. It now stands in the Louvre museum in Paris.

In 1950, more fragments* of the victory goddess were discovered. A few of these were kept in Vienna, Austria. But the head, arms, and the missing pieces of the feet have still not been found.

How would you like to paint or draw Nike? Would you give her arms and a head? Could she have flowing curls, or straight hair rustling in the wind? Would she perhaps wear something on her head? And what might she have in her hands?

4

Something's roaring in the air.

This lady conquers every heart in her flight!
She still looks powerful and stunning today—even without her arms and head.

Her wings and robe may be made of stone, but they're so lifelike that you can almost hear them rustle and flutter in the wind. The goddess Nike has just landed. And she is a very welcome guest. If she shows herself to you, she is sure to bring you a swift victory! The word Nike is Greek for victory. Doesn't the proud and powerful figure seem like triumph itself?

In 1863, French archaeologists* found more than a hundred fragments—or pieces—of a marble sculpture on the Greek island of Samothrace. When they carefully assembled the fragments together, it became clear that they had discovered one of the most important artworks from antiquity!*

People soon wanted to learn the identity of the sculpture. They found that it resembled images of the goddess Nike on ancient Greek coins. This resemblance—along with other clues—helped them determine that the sculpture was an image of the victory goddess.

The Rhodesians* probably created the marble Nike for a shrine, in thanks to the goddess. They had just won a sea battle over the naval forces of Syrian ruler Antiochus III. They placed the victory goddess high up on the prow of a ship in a pool of water.

Title:
  Winged Victory of Samothrace
Artist:
  unknown
Date:
  around 190 BC
Location:
  Louvre, Paris
Material:
  Marble
Size:
  8 ft. (2.45 m) high
Style:
  Hellenistic*

Friedrich Drake,
***Viktoria*, 1864 - 1873**
Victory Column, Berlin

There is also a goddess of victory on the Victory Column in Berlin. Her name is Victoria, the ancient Roman counterpart of the Greek goddess Nike.

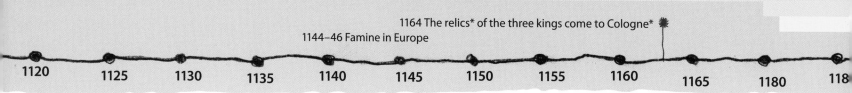

Title:
Shrine of the Three Kings
Artist:
Nicholas of Verdun, various workshops
Date:
around 1190–1230
Location:
Cologne Cathedral, Cologne, Germany
Material:
Oak wood covered by gold, silver, precious stones, beads, and enamel*
Size:
about 4.9 feet (1.5 meters) high, 3 ⅝ ft. (1.1 m) wide, ⅞ in. (2.2 m) long
Style:
Late Romanesque*

Splendor and magnificence on the Rhine

Here gold vies with precious stones, beads, and brilliant enamel.*
Some of the best artists of their era worked on this sumptuous shrine.*

No wonder: It was meant to contain the bones of the three kings! According to the Bible, three wise men from the Orient* visited newborn baby Jesus. These men brought gold and other expensive gifts to Jesus. For hundreds of years, people have called the three visitors kings as well as wise men … even though they were not real kings in the Bible.

On July 23rd of the year 1164, the relics* of the three kings were brought to Cologne. At the time, this German city on the Rhine river was already an important pilgrimage* site. Now that it had the precious bones, Cologne became even more important. Pilgrims poured into the city in such great numbers that, starting in 1248, Cologne Cathedral was built to house the Shrine of the Three Kings.

If you look at the front side of the shrine, you can see young Jesus under the central arch at the bottom. He sits on the lap of his mother, Mary, and greets the three kings … who stand and kneel next to him. Each king presents Jesus with a gift. To the left of the kings someone else—uncrowned but nonetheless very self-confident—has placed himself in this holy scene: King Otto IV of Braunschweig. He donated gold and precious stones for the front of the shrine.*

6

1209 Coronation of Emperor Otto IV*

1248 Start of construction on Cologne Cathedral

Otto IV of Braunschweig around 1180–1218

Nicholas of Verdun, died 1205

1190–1230 *Shrine of the Three Kings*

1190   1195   1200   1205   1215   1220   1225   1230   1235   1240   1245   1250

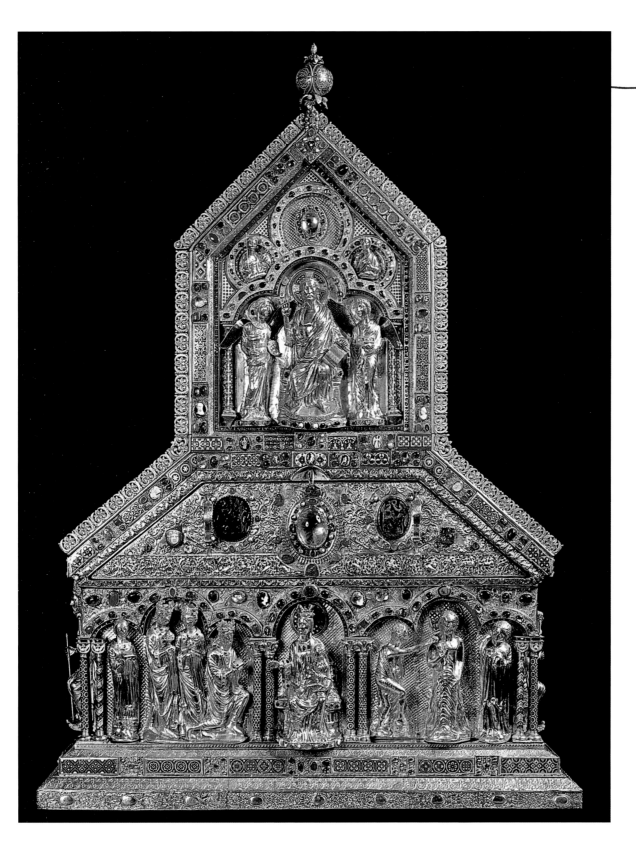

The front side of the shrine*

is the only one made of pure gold. At the top a figure of Christ sits on a throne. Behind the central panel, decorated with precious stones, you can peek inside the shrine to see the relics of the three kings.

The shrine looks like a type of church called a basilica.*

It has two long sides, each with a row of arches on the bottom level and a row on the top. Under each arch sits a little sculpted figure representing a character from the Bible. The bottom row on one side has King Solomon* seated in the middle, while the middle of the other bottom row has King David.* Each king sits in between six of the twelve Old Testament prophets.* These figures look like antique* statues and are probably the work of Nicholas of Verdun. Six of the twelve apostles* sit on the upper row on each side. They may have been made at the workshop of another sculptor. In the middle of each group of apostles is a seated angel.

January 6th is Epiphany, the feast of the three kings. People in Switzerland and France celebrate by baking kings cakes, which have a sweet almond inside. Whoever finds the almond is king for a day and gets to wear a crown of gold paper. You can make a crown like this yourself! Perhaps the decorations from the Shrine of the Three Kings give you ideas for patterns that you can then cut into the paper crown with scissors. The crown will look even more precious if you glue sparkly beads on it.

Two of the three kings are bringing baby Jesus their gifts:

up close you can see how finely detailed the faces and clothing are. The figures almost look like they could speak! Colorful precious stones help make the gold sculptures even more beautiful.

Tip:
The United Nations' UNESCO World Heritage website has a special page on Cologne Cathedral: http://whc.unesco.org/en/list/292. Here you can learn more about the cathedral and even take a digital "tour" of the building on your computer!

580 600 620 640 660 680 700 720 740 760 780 800

According to legend,

Ganesha hurled one of his tusks at the moon when it made fun of his fat belly.

1144–46 Famine in Europe
1190–1230 *Shrine of the Three Kings*

Muhammad bin Tughlug, Sultan (Muslim ruler) of Delhi, around 1300–1351

1206–1526 Muslims rule much of India under the Delhi Sultanate
1248 Start of construction on Cologne Cathedral

| 900 | 1000 | 1100 | 1200 | 1220 | 1240 | 1260 | 1280 | 1300 | 1320 | 1340 | 1360 |

The holy elephant

Friendly, clever, fond of sweets, and pretty fat: that's Ganesha. But more than anything else, he is one of the most beloved gods of the Hindus*. He is believed to bring success, wisdom, and good luck. So many people worship him in temples and seek his blessing before making any important decisions.

Title:
Dancing Ganesha
Artist:
unknown
Date:
10th century
Location:
The Metropolitan Museum of Art, New York
Material:
Red sandstone
Size:
36 in. (91.4 cm) high
20 in. (50.8 cm) wide
Style:
Hindu* art

There are many paintings and sculptures depicting the friendly elephant god. The figure of red sandstone that you see here was carved about a thousand years ago in the province of Madhya Pradesh in central India.

How did Ganesha get his elephant head? According to one story, Ganesha's mother, the goddess Parvati, formed her son herself out of clay and water from the Ganges River—with a human head, of course—and breathed life into him. When her husband, the god Shiva, came home, Ganesha did not want to let him in. After all, the two did not even know each other. The angry Shiva struck off his head! Parvati implored Shiva to save her son, and he promised to give Ganesha the head of the first creature to come by. Ganesha was lucky: it was an elephant, and elephants are strong and thought to be wise.

On days when festivals are held in honor of Ganesha, many Indian children make little figures of the holy elephant out of clay. Would you like to make your own Ganesha?

11

Title:
Great Buddha of Kamakura

Artist:
Ōno-Gorōemon, Tanji-Hisatomo

Date:
1252

Location:
Kōtoku-in, Kamakura, Japan

Material:
Bronze*

Size:
43 13/16 ft. (13.35 m) high
(circumference of thumb:
2 7/8 ft. [0.85 m])

Style:
Buddhist* art

A miracle of serenity

The Great Buddha is peace itself. Nothing can disturb him. Not even a tsunami!

On September 20th of 1498, a huge tidal wave called a tsunami tore away the wooden temple in which the great Buddha was sitting. At that time, this huge sculpture was already 240 years old. Today, it still towers over a Buddhist* temple complex in the city of Kamakura near Tokyo. But it now sits in the open air.

The sculpture is hollow. Whoever wants to can walk in and look at it from the inside. There you can clearly see that the figure is assembled from separate, heavy pieces of bronze—an amazing achievement by the people who made it!

The English author Rudyard Kipling, who wrote The Jungle Book, composed a poem about the Great Buddha of Kamakura in 1892.

"Buddha" means "the enlightened one."

Buddhism* originated in India, and the religion spread to Japan from China and Korea. The posture and face of the Great Buddha of Kamakura appear both peaceful and thoughtful. He seems unconcerned with the everyday problems of the world.

The great Buddha originally sat in a wooden temple.

Since 1489, when a tidal wave destroyed the temple, he has been sitting in the open. Wind and weather have given him his green patina,* and most of his original covering of gold has flaked off. Only in the ears can some of this golden covering still be seen.

Title:
David
Artist:
Michelangelo
Date:
1501–04
Location:
Galleria dell'Accademia,
Florence
Material:
Marble
Size:
17 ft. 11 ¾ in.
(5.48 m) high
(with pedestal)
Style:
Renaissance*

Little big man

This sculpted man is enormous! Yet he represents a character from the Bible—young David—who is only a small boy

The Old Testament* tells how the shepherd boy David used his cleverness and skill to conquer the giant Goliath in a dual. He took aim at Goliath with his slingshot, hitting him on the head with a deadly blow. David later became king of Israel, and he was considered a wise and just ruler. These good qualities made him a role model for future generations.

In 1501, the proud Italian city of Florence wanted a magnificent sculpture of David for their cathedral. It was to be carved out of a single giant block of marble! Only Michelangelo was equal to the task. Not yet thirty years old, he was already one of the most famous sculptors in all of Italy.

When Michelangelo completed his David, the people who first saw it were amazed at its beauty. Many in Florence believed the sculpture shouldn't be placed high up on the cathedral, where it might be hard to see. They felt it should be displayed proudly in the city's main square. David soon found a home in front of Florence's town hall, the Palazzo Vecchio. Today, a copy of the sculpture stands there; the original can be seen in a nearby museum.

Daniele da Volterra,
Michelangelo Buonarroti,
arround1553
Tyler Museum, Haarlem

In this drawing,
Michelangelo is
already an old man.

16

Michelangelo depicts David before the battle,

his slingshot flung casually over his shoulder. In his right hand he already holds the stone. He looks calmly, self-confidently, and with concentration over his left arm into the distance.

Today, a copy of Michelangelo's *David*

stands in the square in front of the Palazzo Vecchio in Florence. The original can be found— protected from wind and weather—in a museum called the Galleria dell'Accademia.

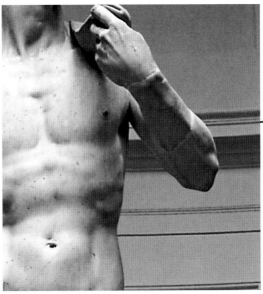

Every single muscle is visible:

this David is in very good shape. People admire him not only as a work of art but also because of his physical beauty.

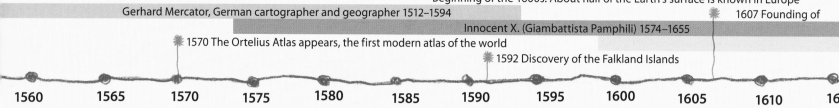

Beginning of the 1600s: About half of the Earth's surface is known in Europe

Gerhard Mercator, German cartographer and geographer 1512–1594

1607 Founding of

Innocent X. (Giambattista Pamphili) 1574–1655

1570 The Ortelius Atlas appears, the first modern atlas of the world

1592 Discovery of the Falkland Islands

1560   1565   1570   1575   1580   1585   1590   1595   1600   1605   1610   161

This figure of the Ganges

reclines on a stone slab. He represents a mighty river that flows through India and Bangladesh. For Hindus,* the Ganges is holy.

Great theater

What a spectacle! There's quite a lot going on here! Everything's flowing and moving.

In the Baroque* era, people loved grand monuments. This was especially true of Pope Innocent V, who came from a wealthy Italian family called the Pamphili. Innocent hired Gian Lorenzo Bernini, a famous sculptor and architect, to build just such a monument in Rome. It would be called the Fountain of the Four Rivers.

Even from a distance, the almost 50-foot-high obelisk* at the center of the fountain is impressive and beautiful. It seems to hover upon Bernini's artificial hill of marble. The obelisk originally came from Egypt. There it stood in a temple for the Egyptian goddess Isis,* which the Roman emperor Domitian had built more than 1,600 years earlier. When the obelisk became part of Bernini's fountain, the artist placed a marble dove on top of it. This bird was an important symbol of the Pamphili family and Pope Innocent V.

Name:
Fountain of the Four Rivers
Artist:
Gian Lorenzo Bernini
Date:
1648–51
Location:
Piazza Navona, Rome
Material:
Travertine* marble
Size:
about 50 feet (15 m) high
Style:
Baroque*

Roman emperor Domitian,

who originally commissioned the obelisk,* had a tribute to himself carved into the obelisk in hieroglyphics.*

The figure representing the Nile

covers its head. At the time, the source of this mighty river was not yet known.

Quiz question:
What four continents were already known in Bernini's time? Which river flows in which continent?
(answer on page 45)

At the base of the obelisk,* Bernini built an artificial rocky hill from pieces of travertine.* He placed four powerful figures of men on top of the hill. They embody great rivers—the Danube, the Nile, the Ganges, and the Rio de la Plata*—from the four known continents of Bernini's day. Surrounding the figures are typical plants and animals from each of the continents. Next to the figure of the Nile, for example, is a lush palm tree—which is common to that river's continent of Africa.

The fountain celebrates nature as God's creation. It also glorifies Pope Innocent X, who at the time ruled as "God's representative on Earth."

The Rio de la Plata*

A fourth male figure

embodies the Danube.

Title:
   The Burghers of Calais
Artist:
   Auguste Rodin
Date:
   1884–95
Location:
   Town square, Calais
Material:
   Cast bronze*
Size:
   7 ft. 2 5/8 in.
   (2.2 m) high,
   7 ft. 8 ½ in.
   (2.35 m) wide,
   5 ft. 10 in.
   (1.78 m) deep
Style:
   Early Modern

A monument steps down from its pedestal

It is the year 1347. The situation of the city of Calais is desperate, even hopeless: the siege by the English has already lasted almost a year.

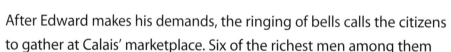

In order to avoid the threatened destruction of his city, the mayor of Calais offers to surrender to the English king Edward III. Edward accepts, but with one condition. Six of Calais' most respected citizens must bring him the keys to their city; and they must be barefoot, dressed in almost nothing but shirts, and with nooses* around their necks. Edward will then hang these six in order to save the city.

After Edward makes his demands, the ringing of bells calls the citizens to gather at Calais' marketplace. Six of the richest men among them volunteer as hostages, led by the elderly Eustache de Saint-Pierre.

This photograph from 1902 shows

Auguste Rodin in his workshop in Meudon, France, surrounded by plaster fragments.*

1889 World Fair in Paris

1895 Exhibition of *The Burghers of Calais* in Calais

1884–95 *The Burghers of Calais*

1914–18 First World War

1939–45 Second World War

1890   1895   1900   1905   1910   1915   1920   1925   1930   1935   1940   1945

The faces, gestures,

 and postures of the men expressively mirror what they are feeling.

Around 550 years later, the city of Calais wanted to erect a monument to the leader of the brave group. It commissioned the celebrated sculptor Auguste Rodin. But Rodin did not want to create a traditional monument for a single chosen hero. Instead, he depicted all six of the citizens. They form a closely united group, although Rodin represents each figure with an individual personality. He arranges them not just one beside the other, but in a circular movement that emphasizes their common willingness to sacrifice themselves. But most unusual of all, Rodin wants his monument placed at ground level, not raised up on a high pedestal. He wants the viewer to encounter the figures at eye level. At first, Rodin's clients were not at all happy with this idea. Yet people soon came to admire this great work of art.

In the Musée Rodin

there is a plaster cast of this famous group of figures. It´s from 1889.

Tip:
Twelve copies of The Burghers of Calais were made. The German artist Candida Höfer photographed all twelve at their locations throughout the world.

Besides Calais, the other locations are: Copenhagen (Denmark), Ny Carlsberg Glyptothek; Mariemont (Belgium), Musée Royal; London, Garden of Parliament; Philadelphia (USA), Rodin Museum; Paris, Musée Rodin; Basel (Switzerland), Kunstmuseum; Washington, D.C., Hirshhorn Museum and Sculpture Garden; Tokyo, National Museum of Western Art; Pasadena (USA), Norton Simon Museum of Art; New York, Metropolitan Museum of Art; Seoul (South Korea), Rodin Gallery

The story of the six burghers of Calais did not end tragically. Upon the request of the English queen, the six men were spared by the king. But the war between France and England would go on for more than another hundred years, giving the conflict its name: the Hundred Years' War.

What were the lives of the six burghers of Calais like? Where did they get their courage in the face of possible death? Write your own version of their stories!

Why is the little monkey baring his teeth?

Is he having fun teasing the big animal? Or could he be afraid? It's hard to tell exactly what kind of animal the larger one is: maybe the head belongs to a jackal or a hyena, … or what would you guess? Underneath you can see the grip for the dancer to hold the mask.

Tip:
You can learn more about African masks in Christine Stelzig's book Can You Spot The Leopard? African Masks (Adventures in Art), 1997.

Companion in a new life

Pretty fearless, this agile little monkey. He's right on top of the larger animal's head and holds on tight to his ears.

An unknown African artist made this sculpture, called an Mbala mask, for a great celebration. When the boys of a Yaka* village reach a certain age, they take part in a ceremony to join their village's community of adults. The ceremony lasts several days, and many masked dances are included in the program. At the end of the festival, the most beautiful and lavish mask is brought forward—the Mbala mask. It is meant to surprise and delight everyone in the celebration.

The artist of this mask has carved the two animals separately and fastened them together. Thick handfuls of plant fibers, which look somewhat like a lion's mane, have been attached to the head of the larger animal.

Typically, the painted patterns on masks such as this one have been used for many generations within a village. The paints are produced from colored soils and plants.

Many modern European artists, including Pablo Picasso, loved African art. They used images resembling those from African art in their own paintings and sculptures.

Title:
Mbala mask
Artist:
unknown
Date:
Early 20th century
Location:
Museum Rietberg, Zurich
Material:
Wood, raffia, paint
Size:
21 2/3 in. (55 cm) high
Style:
Yaka* workshop, Congo region (Zaire)

29

1914–1918 First World War

Auguste Rodin 1840–1917

Constantin Brâncuşi 1876–1957

1904 Brâncuşi arrives in Paris

1916 Fighting in Târgu Jiu during the First World War

1929 Claes Oldenb[...]

1937–1938 *Endless Column*

1884–1895 *The Burghers of Calais*

| 1860 | 1870 | 1880 | 1890 | 1900 | 1905 | 1910 | 1915 | 1920 | 1925 | 1930 | 193[5] |

The basic shape

that Brâncuşi used to assemble his Endlesss Column is about the size of a person.

Tip:
When Brâncuşi received the commission for the monument in Târgu Jiu, he had already been a famous sculptor for a long time in Paris. At Paris's Centre Georges Pompidou museum, you can visit a rebuilt version of the artist's old workshop.

Quiz question:
Look carefully at the basic shape of the column; it is made up of two identical smaller shapes. Can you draw the basic shape on a piece of paper? Maybe you can figure out what those smaller shapes might be.

(Answer on page 45)

1939–1945 Second World War

orn

Robert Smithson 1938–1973

1982–83 *Stravinsky Fountain*

Jean Tinguely 1925–1991

1964 *Giant Tooth Paste Tube*

1970 *Spiral Jetty*

1940   1945   1950   1955   1960   1965   1970   1975   1980   1985   1990   2000

Towards the sky

It goes up and up and up ... and could go on forever,
up towards the sky!

Constantin Brâncuși's Endless Column may look endlessly tall, but it's not.
It's made up of seventeen hollow iron shapes stacked one on top of the
other. All the shapes in the column are identical, except for the one on the
bottom and the one on the top. The bottom shape is slightly shorter than
the ones in the middle, while the top shape is half the size of the middle
shapes. This smaller top shape makes the column look like it could go
upward forever, especially when the column is viewed from its base.

The Endless Column is part of a memorial site in Târgu Jiu, Romania. This
special site is dedicated to the memory of Romanian soldiers who died
fighting the Germans in the First World War. Brâncuși had lived in the city
as a boy. His column seems to reach upwards to heaven, like the souls of
the dead.

Brâncuși had worked out the idea of the Endless Column in 1918.
Photographs of his workshop show the sculpture in several versions,
carved out of wood or formed in plaster.

Title:
 Endless Column
Artist:
 Constantin Brâncuși
Date:
 1937–39
Location:
 Târgu Jiu, Romania
Material:
 Cast iron*
 with yellowish
 metal coating
Size:
 98 ft. 5 $\frac{1}{8}$ in.
 (30 m) high
Style:
 Abstraction*

Title:
Giant Toothpaste Tube
Artist:
Claes Oldenburg
Date:
1964
Location:
The Cleveland
Museum of Art,
Cleveland
Material:
Canvas,* metal,
polyester, kapok
Size:
About 16 $^{15}/_{16}$ in. (43
cm) high,
25 $^{9}/_{16}$ in. (65 cm) wide,
66 $^{1}/_{8}$ in. (168 cm) long
Style:
Pop Art

Out of daily life and into the museum

Does something like this belong in a museum?
A squeezed-out tube of toothpaste?

Yes, thought Claes Oldenburg. The American artist designed an over-sized tube of toothpaste, had it sewn out of canvas,* and then stuffed it with kapok—a plant fiber normally used as a stuffing for mattresses and furniture. His Giant Toothpaste Tube is thus soft and flexible, and it can be draped and bent in various ways. The material used to create this artwork, as well as its giant size and its location in a museum, make the object look strange to us … even though it closely resembles something that we use every day.

🌟 1963 Assassination of US president John F. Kennedy
🌟 1964 *Giant Tooth Paste Tube*
Niki de Saint Phalle 1930–2002
🌟 1970 *Spiral Jetty*   1982–83 *Strawinsky Fountain*
2004–2006 *Cloud Gate*

63   1964   1970   1975   1980   1985   1990   1995   2000   2005   2010   2015

In the 1960s, many sculptors and painters decided to make art out of objects that could be found in any supermarket. They wanted people to look at these well-known, or "popular," objects in new ways. Their artistic movement came to be called Pop Art. "Pop" stands for "popular." Claes Oldenburg produced other kinds of "popular" art objects, including those that looked like hamburgers or ice cream cones. He even set up an entire exhibition of Pop Art objects, calling it The Store.

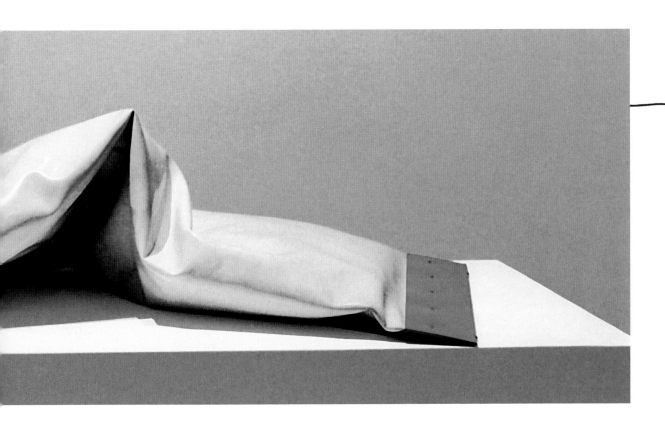

Doesn't the tube here look like a person lying down

with her legs bent? Sculptors have been carving such figures for hundreds of years, and the figures are often women. Perhaps Claes Oldenburg is poking a bit of fun at this traditional kind of sculpture.

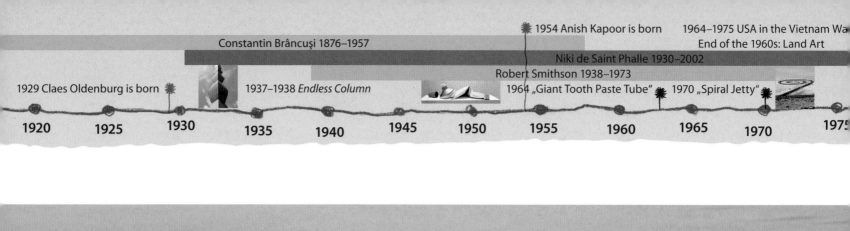

1954 Anish Kapoor is born   1964–1975 USA in the Vietnam Wa

Constantin Brâncuşi 1876–1957   End of the 1960s: Land Art

Niki de Saint Phalle 1930–2002

Robert Smithson 1938–1973

1929 Claes Oldenburg is born   1937–1938 *Endless Column*   1964 „Giant Tooth Paste Tube"   1970 „Spiral Jetty"

1920   1925   1930   1935   1940   1945   1950   1955   1960   1965   1970   1975

Extra-extra-large sculpture

This sculpture is so huge that it can be seen from space. It was built up out of 6,550 tons of earth and stones, the weight of about a thousand African elephants.

Of course the artist could not move these enormous materials himself. He hired Bob Phillips—a man with experience constructing large buildings—to help him create his artwork. The earth and stones were brought in from the surrounding area, and the materials were piled into the Great Salt Lake with a dump truck. This lake lies in the state of Utah in the United States. Even today, Smithson's work of art can only be reached by driving on rough country roads that lead to the shore of the lake. Visitors can walk upon the Spiral Jetty,* but the work is sometimes flooded. Art that is made to fit into the open landscape, like Smithson's spiral, is called Land Art. The landscape itself becomes part of such art.

You can make you own spiral by collecting stones, small branches, or leaves; and then placing them in a spiral shape in your yard. Be sure to get your parents' permission first!

Title:
 Spiral Jetty
Artist:
 Robert Smithson
Date:
 1970
Location:
 Rozel Point,
 Great Salt Lake, USA
Material:
 Basalt rock,* earth
 Size of the strip:
 14 ft. 11 $^{15}/_{16}$ in.
 (4.57 m) wide,
 1500 ft. (457.2 m) long
Style:
 Land Art

Tip:
Many photographs of Spiral Jetty can be found at the website http://scenicutah.com/spiral-jetty/spiraljetty.php. The work of art even has its own website. There you can also see the film produced by Robert Smithson about the making of Spiral Jetty (www.spiraljetty.org.). You can learn more about the artist at www.robertsmithson.com. Photographs taken from space can be found at http://virtualglobetrotting.com/map/29348.

For several years, Spiral Jetty disappeared under the surface of the Great Salt Lake.

After a long draught the jetty reappeared. Since 1999, the work has been in the care of the Dia Art Foundation. To keep the Spiral Jetty from being submerged again, some people have suggested that more stones and earth be heaped onto it. But would the artist, who died in 1973 in a place crash, have wanted this?

Quiz question:
The spiral is a form found often in nature. Can you think of any spiral shapes from the plant or animal kingdoms? Why has the Spiral Jetty turned white?

(answers on page 45)

Water ballet with the firebird

Title:
 Stravinsky Fountain
Artist:
 Niki de Saint Phalle,
 Jean Tinguely
Date:
 1982–83
Location:
 Place Igor Stravinski,
 Paris
Material of the mechanical sculptures:
 Aluminum, steel,
 asphalt paint
Material of the figures:
 Polyester,
 17 electrical motors
Size of the fountain:
 118 ft. 1 $^{5}/_{16}$ in.
 (36 m) long,
 54 ft. 1 $^{5}/_{8}$ in.
 (16.5 m) wide,
 13 ¾ in. (.35 m) high
Style:
 New Realism*

In the middle of Paris, just behind the Centre Georges Pompidou museum, the firebird directs a cast of strange mechanical figures and brightly colored fairy-tale creatures.

The fountain was made by the artist team of Jean Tinguely and Niki de Saint Phalle. Jean had become famous making sculptures that could move mechanically; while Niki was known for her rich, colorfully painted figures, especially her Nanas.* When creating the fountain, Niki de Saint Phalle made skeleton-like "frameworks" of stainless steel and metal wire for her figures. She covered these frameworks with a "skin" of plastic, which was then painted. Niki and Jean dedicated their fountain to the Russian-born music composer Igor Stravinsky. In the early 1900s, Stravinsky had composed many great ballets for his friend Sergei Diaghilev, who led a company of ballet dancers called the Ballets Russes. One of Stravinski's ballets was called The Firebird, and it was based on Russian folk tales.

**The artist
Niki de Saint Phalle,**

photographed in 1980

The firebird dominates the center of the Strawinsky Fountain.

The water shoots around his head like sparks.

The firebird lives with the evil magician Kastschej. One day Prince Ivan goes hunting and catches the firebird. The bird asks the prince to release him and promises him one of his feathers in exchange. This feather will help Ivan in freeing thirteen maidens whom the magician is keeping imprisoned in his garden. Among the maidens is a princess whom Prince Ivan loves. When the magician finds out what has happened, he sends demons to kill Ivan. Once again the firebird helps the prince: he makes the demons dance to his music and then puts them to sleep with a song. Finally he shows Ivan an egg in which the soul of the magician is kept. The prince destroys the egg, breaking the power of the magician. The maidens are then freed, and the prince gets his princess.

The cuddly elephant

with his ears sticking out can spout water especially well.

The snake—also affectionately called "the corkscrew"—

can dance like a ballerina!

What do you think a firebird looks like? You can paint it with watercolors, glue it together with colored paper, or form it from colored clay or wax. Or you can make a framework out of sheets of wire called wire mesh, and then cover it with papier mâché. You can get the wire mesh at any hardware store. To make the papier mâché, stir wallpaper paste in a large bowl according to the instructions on the package. Then take some old newspapers and tear them into small pieces, dip them in the paste, and lay them on the wire mesh in several layers. When the paper is dry, you can paint it. First make a coat of white paint, and then use colorful watercolors to paint designs on top of the white coat.

Visitors can walk underneath the roughly 12-foot-high arch made by Cloud Gate.

From underneath, visitors look into the "navel" of the sculpture. Here the surface looks like it has been pushed inward to create a funnel-like shape. Images on the navel's surface appear broken-up and distorted, as pictures do in a kaleidoscope.

The sculpture's curved surface

acts as a funny mirror, entertaining the people who stroll in the park.

Bridge between heaven and earth

A shiny sculpture seems to float in Chicago's Millennium Park … as if it had just come down from the sky.

A drop of quicksilver* inspired Indian artist Anish Kapoor to make this artwork, called Cloud Gate. Quicksilver is a shiny, reflective metal that, like Cloud Gate, appears almost weightless. The appearance of Cloud Gate changes from second to second; for the reflections of the skyscrapers, clouds, and other objects around it change on its surface according to the viewer's position, the weather, and the time of day. When light hits the sculpture in a certain way, Cloud Gate almost looks like it has become part of the sky.

Cloud Gate weighs 99 tons and was assembled from 168 steel plates, all curved differently. In order to make the seams between the plates invisible, a special company polished it in five different stages. The sculpture now truly shines. However, its surface needs to be cleaned and maintained constantly. People of Chicago, by the way, have given Cloud Gate the affectionate and funny nickname "the bean"—because of the work's bean-like shape.

Title:
Cloud Gate
Artist:
Anish Kapoor
Date:
2004–06
Location:
Millennium Park, Chicago
Material:
Stainless steel
Size:
33 ft. (10 m) high,
66 ft. (20 m) long,
42 ft. (13 m) wide
Style:
Post Minimalism*

Tip:
You can find photos of Cloud Gate from various angles and at different times of day at www.flickr.com. Enter "cloud gate" in the search field.

The reflections in Cloud Gate are particularly impressive and attract many photographers. Maybe in your town or on your street you can find reflecting surfaces that mirror their surroundings. Take a camera with you when you go.

Glossary

ABSTRACTION Abstract artists create art out of shapes and colors, rather than depicting people and things exactly as they appear in real life.

ANTIQUE The time of the ancient Greeks and Romans (around 800 BC to AD 500). The term comes from the Latin word antiquus, which means "old."

APOSTLE (Greek: "messenger") The people whom Jesus Christ asked to spread his teachings. These teachings became the basis for Christianity.

ARCHAEOLOGIST A person who studies the distant past. Archaeologists search for objects and other evidence of long-ago human culture, often by digging underground.

BAROQUE A period of art history from around 1600 to the middle of the 1700s. In the Baroque era, architects had a fondness for creating curved shapes. The name "baroque" comes from barocco, the Portuguese word for "misshaped pearl".

BASALT A dark gray or black stone made of hardened magma, a substance that explodes or flows out of volcanoes during eruptions.

BASILICA In antiquity,* a law or market hall. The name was later adopted for church buildings in which the interior was divided into three or more parts (aisles) by rows of columns. The central aisle, or nave, is higher than the side aisles and has windows above the aisles.

BRONZE CASTING A plaster or clay model is used to make a hollow shape into which melted bronze (a mixture of copper and tin, often with other metals) is poured.

BUDDHISM A religion founded by Buddha Siddhartha (around 560 BC to around 480 BC) in India. Buddhists believe in reincarnation, or the cycle of being reborn after death in the form of another person or creature. By achieving "enlightenment"—a state of peace and profound understanding of oneself—a person can end his or her own cycle of reincarnation.

CANVAS A textile produced from the fibers of the flax plant, used as a painting surface for pictures.

CAST IRON This material consists of iron and a small amount of carbon. It is poured, or cast, into molds and hardened into specific shapes.

DAVID The Biblical King of Israel and Judea (around 1000 to 960 BC) who, while still a young boy, fought against the giant Goliath.

ENAMEL A covering for metal objects that is made from melted colored glass. This covering both protects the object and makes it more beautiful. Enamel is applied as a powder and then melted in enamel ovens.

HELLENISTIC A style of art from between around 330 BC to 30 BC, when Greek (or "Hellenic") culture was adopted in many parts of Europe, northern Africa, and western Asia.

HIEROGLYPHS A system of writing that uses pictures instead of words. The ancient Egyptians produced famous hieroglyphs.

HINDUISM A religion originally developed in India. Hindus believe in reincarnation, or the rebirth after death into another person or creature.

ISIS An Egyptian goddess of motherhood, magic, and healing.

LATE ROMANESQUE Last period of the Romanesque, one of the artistic eras of the Middle Ages in Europe. During the Middle Ages, most art was made for the Christian church. The late Romanesque period lasted from around 1125 to 1250. Its name comes from the shape of the arches found in Romanesque churches. Such arches resemble those from ancient Roman architecture.

JETTY A structure built in a lake or sea to protect the nearby land from flooding, or to create a safe place to keep ships.

NANA The name Niki de St. Phalle gave to her colorful sculptures.

NEW REALISM An art movement that lasted from the middle of the 1950s into the 1970s. Like Pop Art, it was interested in using objects of everyday life in surprising and exciting ways.

NOOSE A rope used to hang someone by the neck.

OBELISK A tall stone pillar that becomes narrower toward the top and has a tip shaped like a pyramid.

OLD TESTAMENT The religious text containing the Tanakh, the holy writings of Judaism. The Old and New Testaments form the two parts of the Bible.

ORIENT The name that Europeans gave to lands in what is now Asia.

PATINA When certain metals are exposed to air and weather; they develop a thin, colored layer—sometimes called a patina—on their surface. Copper often develops a green patina.

PILGRIMAGE Travel to a place of religious importance. Many pilgrims take their journey so that God will forgive their sins or heal them from a disease.

POST MINIMALISM The name of an art movement that developed from another movement called Minimalism. Minimalist art uses simple shapes of plastic and other industrial materials. These works are often produced by machine and are based on the artists' designs. Post Minimalists work with similar materials, but they typically use them in a more playful manner in their art.

PROPHET (Greek: "speaker," "admonisher") Someone who proclaims the word of God. Prophets often criticize people in their own communities for their lack of faithfulness to God's teachings.

QUICKSILVER ("living silver") Silvery, shiny, and very poisonous metal that is a liquid at room temperature. At cold temperatures, it forms smooth, bean-shaped drops.

RELIC (Latin: "remains") Body parts or objects from a saint or other important religious person.

RENAISSANCE (French: "rebirth") During the Renaissance, the art of antiquity* was closely studied. This art influenced the work of Renaissance architects, painters, and sculptors.

RHODESIANS Inhabitants of the island of Rhodes, which is now part of Greece.

RIO DE LA PLATA (Spanish: "Silver River") The combination of two of the largest rivers in South America, the Paraná and the Uruguay. The Rio de la Plata is over 186 miles long.

SHRINE Box or chest for keeping relics.*

SOLOMON Son of David, and King of Israel probably from 965 to 926 BC.

TRAVERTINE ("lapis tiburtinus": stone from Tivoli) A yellowish or brownish limestone.

YAKA ("the strong ones") An ethnic group that lives in southwestern Africa, in what are now the countries of Angola and the Democratic Republic of the Congo.

Answers to quiz questions:

p. 22:   Europe – Danube
Africa – Nile
Asia – Ganges
America – Rio de la Plata

p. 30:   The basic shape is two pyramids with their tips cut off.

p. 34:   A few examples from nature are snail's shells, fern leaves, tornados.
The *Spiral Jetty* has become covered with a layer of salt.

Library of Congress Control Number: 2009942194; British Library Cataloguing-in-Publication Data: a catalogue record for this book is available from the British Library; Deutsche Nationalbibliothek holds a record of this publication in the Deutsche Nationalbibliografie; detailed bibliographical data can be found under: http://d-nb.ddb.de

Prestel books are available worldwide. Please contact your nearest bookseller or one of the above addresses for information concerning your local distributor.

Front cover: Details taken from works by Michelangelo (p.17), Oldenburg (p.32), Smithson (p.35)
Frontispiece: Niki de Saint Phalle, Stravinsky Fountain, Firebird, 1982-83

Picture credits:
akg-images, Berlin: pp. 32/33; Hans Himmelheber: p. 29; Albert und Irmgard Ernstmeier-Hirmer: pp. 8-9, 19; The New York Times/Redux/laif: pp. 34, 36/37; LOOK: pp. 14/15, 18; The Metropolitan Museum of Art/Art Resource/Scala, Florenz: p. 10; Musée Rodin, Paris: pp. 26-27; Rheinisches Bildarchiv: p. 7; Larry Rivers: p. 38; Peter Stepan: pp. 39-41

Prestel a member of Verlagsgruppe Random House GmbH

Prestel Verlag
Königinstraße 9
80539 München

www.prestel.de

Prestel Publishing Ltd.
4, Bloomsbury Place,
London WC1A 2QA

Prestel Publishing
900 Broadway, Suite 603,
New York, NY 10003

www.prestel.com

Translated from the German by: Cynthia Hall
Editorial direction: Doris Kutschbach, Andrea Weißenbach
Copyedited by: Brad Finger
Design and layout: Michael Schmölzl, agenten.und.freunde, Munich
Production: Astrid Wedemeyer
Art direction: Cilly Klotz
Origination: Reproline Mediateam, Munich
Printing and Binding: Tlačiasne BB, spol. sr. o.

FSC
Mix
Produktgruppe aus vorbildlich bewirtschafteten Wäldern, kontrollierten Herkünften und Recyclingholz oder -fasern
Product group from well-managed forests, controlled sources and recycled wood or fibre
Zert.-Nr. SGS-COC-004238
www.fsc.org
© 1996 Forest Stewardship Council

Verlagsgruppe Random House FSC-DEU-0100
The FSC-certified paper Opus Praximatt produced by mill Condat has been supplied by Deutsche Papier

Printed in Slovak Republic

ISBN 978-3-7913-7010-1